I0160656

Living Our Values:
Ethics in Action

Edward L. Felton, Jr.

Ethicos Press

In Support of Valuable Living

Ethicos Press

Living Our Values: Ethics in Action

ISBN: Softcover 978-1-936912-16-2

Copyright © 2011 by Edward L. Felton, Jr.

All rights reserved. No part of this book may be reproduced or transmitted in any form or by any means, electronic or mechanical, including photocopying, recording, or by any information storage and retrieval system, without permission in writing from the publisher.

This book was printed in the United States of America.

To order additional copies of this book, contact:

Ethicos Press
1-423-475-7308
www.ethicospress.com

Ethicos Press is an imprint of Parson's Porch & Company (PP&C) in Cleveland, Tennessee. PP&C is an innovative non-profit organization which raises money by publishing books of noted authors, representing all genres. All donations from contributors and profits from publishing go to help the poor.

Dedication

To Kate, Mitchell, Gray, Kel and Alex—

Your boundless curiosity, your inspiring resilience, your contagious enthusiasm, and your deep reservoirs of joy enrich the life of your grandfather in incalculable ways.

Acknowledgments

Living Our Values: Ethics in Action is a product of the Walsh Ethics Initiative of the Mason School of Business at The College of William and Mary. This program was established and endowed by Patrick and Margaret Walsh, both graduates of the College. Mr. Walsh had a distinguished career as a senior executive at Merrill Lynch.

The author gratefully acknowledges the support of administrative and professional colleagues and graduate students at the Mason School of Business. Particular thanks are owed to Mason School Dean Larry Pulley, Associate Dean Jon Krapfl, and Tom Rideout, Senior Associate Director of Mason's Accounting Programs.

Graduate students Brittany Scopa, Ned Marcalus, Ryan Tower, Eric O'Brien, Sammy Hamididdin, Jill Mazur, Mike Lamb, and Larry Van Sant had core impact on the focus and structure of the book and conducted both field and library research. Britanny made meaningful contributions in particular to the development of the following cases: "Cheating at McDaniel College," "Rick Reynolds Needs a Signature," "Debra Gotfried and Ritalin," "Molly Graham's Situation," "Angie's Book," "Mark Pittman's Party," and "Voting for the First Time." Ned made contributions to the case "A Second Chance for John O'Brien;" Eric, to the case "The Whiterock Football Team;" Sammy, to the case "An Intern's Dilemma;" Jill, to the case "Four Seniors at Lafayette High;" Mike, to the case "T & T Landscaping;" and Larry, to the case "What's the Point?"

Selected data for the case "A Tough Call" came from an article in the September 28, 2010, issue of *USA Today*, page 1A. Data for the case study "Barlow Manufacturing" was derived in part from "Alabama Could Join States That Require Drivers to Know English," an article that appeared in *USA Today*, December 29, 2005, page 3A. Sources of data for Exhibit Two in the case study "Four Seniors at Lafayette High" were the Bureau of Labor Statistics, American Institute for Economic Research, and the College Board Advocacy and Policy Center.

Management cases are created for students, and it is important that they validate the work's true worth. Each case has been tested on numerous occasions in classroom settings. The input of students has been invaluable in helping to refine the focus and in validating the relevance of the cases. I am most grateful to the students for their insights and engaging enthusiasm in discussing the issues and challenges of living one's values.

Kimberly Reeves' fingerprints are found throughout the book. My thanks to her for her supportive attitude and energies and especially for her careful proofreading.

To my daughter, Kimber Felton, goes my thanks for her insightful ideas, her discerning eye for design, and her abiding attention to detail. The book is much the better for her contributions and strong support.

To Frank Dooley goes my deep thanks and appreciation for his keen insights, professional skills, and great patience in shaping the final product. An author could not have had a finer partner as editor.

My deepest appreciation goes to Patrick and Margaret Walsh. I have learned much from them, and their lessons and perspectives are found throughout the volume. In the most profound sense, they have been partners in this endeavor and will be partners with all who are touched by this project. To them, I acknowledge my gratitude and affection.

Table of Contents

Jane Merkley is a freshman at McDaniel College. While studying in the school library late one night, Jane encounters two classmates, Alap Bheda and Deepinder Sweeta, who appear to be cheating on a take-home calculus exam. Jane does not want to be a snitch, but the school's honor code requires that she report the incident. She does not know what to do.

Rick Reynolds, a new student at Lincoln High School, is caught by his math teacher allowing three classmates to copy his answers to a pop quiz. The teacher sends a note about the incident home with Rick for his father to sign. Rick is in a quandary. If Rick's father sees the note, he likely will prohibit Rick from trying out for the basketball team, denying him this opportunity to make new friends at his new school. Rick ponders whether he should forge his father's signature. No one is likely to know.

Debra Gotfried is the valedictorian of her senior class. As she waits to give the address at her high school graduation, she sees in the audience star football running back Brett Jones. Debra recalls that Brett was dismissed from the school's football team last fall for using performance enhancers. Debra's grades and overall academic performance improved significantly after she was introduced to Ritalin by a friend during her freshman year. She has continued to use the drug and now wonders, as she looks at Brett, if she is also guilty of using performance enhancing substances to achieve her academic honor.

High school junior Molly Graham discovers that she is pregnant. She does not know what to do. Her parents are opposed to abortion. If she chooses to have the baby, she will be required by school board policy to transfer to an alternative school until the baby is born. Not only would this take her away from her friends, including her boyfriend, it would also likely force her to defer her lifelong dream of becoming a nurse.

Rachael Gifford's friend and classmate, Angie Wilson, is moving to Florida. As a keepsake and memento of her high school friendships, Angie has created a book in which her friends answer a series of questions that she has posed. Some of the questions are benign, but some deal with complex topics, such as sexual and drug experiences. The book is confiscated by a teacher, and copies are sent to the parents of the students who contributed to the book. This includes Rachael's mother. Now Rachael and her mother must decide how to address issues involving trust, privacy, and the mother-daughter relationship.

6 MARK PITTMAN'S PARTY 47

Mark Pittman, a 17 year old high school senior, is joining the Army immediately after graduation. He wants to host a party to celebrate his graduation and impending departure for boot camp. Mark thinks that having some beer at the party would lighten the mood for him and his buddies. Mark wonders about being old enough to go to war but yet not old enough to drink legally. He is considering asking his parents to provide beer for the party, but this could create both legal and ethical issues for them.

7 A SECOND CHANCE FOR JOHN O'BRIEN 53

John O'Brien is a junior at The Buckley School. He is seen by a teacher standing with three of his band mates near an open window in the school's Performing Arts Center. One of the other boys is holding a marijuana pipe. The Buckley School's honor code states that merely being in the presence of someone who is using drugs violates school policy and requires the immediate expulsion by the headmaster. John is a scholarship student who was raised in the inner city by his grandmother. He has an exemplary record at Buckley: a 4.0 student, a star athletic, and a gifted musician. If the headmaster expels John, it is unlikely that John's dreams of a college scholarship will be fulfilled. If he does not expel John, it will appear that he is not upholding the school's nearly 150 year old honor code and is giving John preferential treatment.

8   THE WHITEROCK FOOTBALL TEAM

Trent Miller, co-captain of the undefeated Whiterock University football team, observes star running back and team co-captain Go-Go Gonzales in a local restaurant drinking a beer while having dinner with his parents. This is a violation of team rules and requires that Trent report what he has seen to Coach Gary Mercer. This will certainly lead to Go-Go's suspension from the team. If Go-Go is suspended, Whiterock will likely lose its final game of the season, shutting them out of any post-season play.

9   AN INTERN'S DILEMMA

Suzanne Patel is completing an expense report which includes the costs of attending a social event hosted by Baath & Thomas, her summer employer. She used public transportation to travel to the event. Tony Hughes, a fellow intern and friend, observes Suzanne filling out the expense report in which she states her transportation costs as being under five dollars. He tells Suzanne that she should indicate that she drove to the event and paid for parking, which will make her an extra forty dollars. And "no one will ever know."

Brad, who has recently turned 18, is voting for the first time today. As he waits in line to vote, he discovers that there is a proposal on the ballot to legalize and tax the sale of small quantities of marijuana for recreational use. Brad is concerned about the possible health risks associated with the use of the drug. But he also understands the possible benefits that could flow from its legalization. Brad faces the challenge of deciding how to vote on this important issue.

Katherine McCoy is a member of the state legislature which currently is considering a much debated bill banning cell phone use while driving. The vote, which is scheduled to take place soon, will be very close. Evidence shows that cell phone use causes highway accidents and injuries. Yet many people, including her husband, who is a real estate agent, and her daughter, oppose the bill. Katherine must decide how she will cast her vote.

Tyler Taylor, a young entrepreneur, has been asked by Chip Green, one of his employees, for a personal loan to prevent the repossession of his wife's vehicle. Tyler does not believe in loaning employees money. Yet Chip, a family friend since childhood, is one of his best workers and manages his top performing landscaping team. Tyler wonders if, in this one instance, he should make an exception to his informal policy of making no loans to employees. Chip is, after all, a friend and highly valued employee.

Charles (Chuck) Barlow is president of Barlow Manufacturing Company. Approximately forty percent of Barlow's hourly employees are immigrants, mainly from Mexico and Central America. As Chuck exits company headquarters one morning on the way to a business appointment, he is unexpectedly confronted by a local television reporter who asks for his views on whether the state should offer driver's license exams in languages other than English. He must decide quickly how to respond.

Northampton County, New Jersey, has a growing Middle Eastern population. David Stewart, a member of the county school board and a local businessman, is asked by his daughter Meredith why she and her classmates do not get out of school for her Muslim friend's holy days. At the next school board meeting, David raises the issue of whether the school system should recognize as official school holidays the Muslim holy days as it does Christian and Jewish holy days. The issue creates a lively discussion among board members who decide to adjourn and revisit the issue at its next meeting.

15   FOUR SENIORS AT LAFAYETTE HIGH   105

Four friends, rising seniors at Lafayette High, have vague plans about what they want to do after graduation. They decide to attend a career seminar hosted by their high school. At the seminar they receive information about various career options. More importantly, they are challenged to think through their definitions of what constitutes "a successful life." As they drive to McDonald's afterwards, the four friends discuss the issues presented at the seminar, issues that suddenly have fresh and pressing relevance to them.

16   WHAT'S THE POINT?   119

William Hargrave has lived a life of solid accomplishments and high achievement. He graduated *summa cum laude* from college, had a successful five years in the Army, graduated from business school, and accepted a prized job offer in the financial industry. At his job, William has received a number of promotions and bonuses for his performance. He recently married his long-time girlfriend, Heather. William's life appears to be the very model of the American success story. He has fulfilled all of the life goals he had set for himself as a very young man. Yet, a vast void and growing unhappiness are present in his life. He wonders, "What's the point?"

From the Author to the Reader

Living Our Values: Ethics in Action focuses on life. It is a book filled with situations in which people must determine relevant facts, confront choices, and then make decisions. This requires analyzing specific sets of facts and circumstances to determine plausible alternatives and then making decisions that result in optimal choices. While hard facts and unique circumstances are vital drivers in the final decision making, there are also internal considerations, notably the individual's own values, that are keys to successful outcomes.

Much like the people described in the cases, your decisions and life actions are at the core of who you are. Values influence and shape your choices. Values define and drive your passions. Values are at the core of how you choose to invest your time, talents, and energies. Values determine the choices you make in your personal and professional life.

The modern global community, inflected by a technological revolution, evolves at a breathtaking pace as it grows increasingly complex. Our daily lives are influenced by events and trends that may occur far from our communities geographically, but which nevertheless have an impact on us in myriad ways that are difficult, if not impossible, to anticipate. News, information, and products and services flow nearly unfettered among nations. So do ideas about who we are and what is required of us to live meaningful lives.

Your peers, colleagues, and teachers often have backgrounds and life experiences that are very different from yours. As a result, so are their values and their vision of life and the world.

The cases in this book are about people who are confronting situations that require difficult decisions. Since these cases are derived from real-world experiences, personal and institutional names, locations, and selected other data have been changed.

Some of the cases concern personal and social issues. Other cases focus on choices in business or other organizational environments.

The final two cases deal with career choices. How you choose to invest your talents professionally is among the most challenging ethical decisions you will face in life. Your choice of career determines to a great extent the scope and impact that your core values will have on the various communities in which you choose to participate.

It serves us well to note that from a historical perspective, having a career choice is a relatively new phenomenon. Throughout history, most humans were destined to do exactly what their parents did. The concept of career choice is new to us, and it carries special responsibilities.

Some of you will read this book as an individual adventure. The case studies will provide you with a personal intellectual experience in thinking about modern ethical dilemmas. You will read each case, analyze the issues, and reach your conclusions without discussion with or interventions by others.

Others of you will read this book as part of a class assignment. Your individual preparation and thinking about the cases and their issues will be accompanied by discussions with others.

Regardless of which situation applies to you, do make an effort to approach the cases with an open mind and an analytical perspective. It is an immediate experience to encounter ethical cases derived from real-world situations. As you approach each case, keep this one question uppermost in your mind: "If I were in this situation, what would I do?"

As this suggests, dealing with the cases effectively is a highly interactive experience. You need to place yourself immediately in the role of the decision-maker in the case, seeking to understand the situation from his or her perspective. Read the cases actively. Keep a pen or pencil in your hand, marking salient facts and recording your reactions and insights.

The cases are laid out in a format that encourages active interaction between you and the case situations. On the right of the texts of the cases are spaces for you to record notes indicated by the icon of the quill and inkwell.

In considering each case, do not seek a quick answer. Begin by focusing on the issues; then carefully identify and consider your options. Think about the bases for your decisions. Try to determine the values that are driving your decision-making. They represent many sources: family values, the culture of the community in which you were raised, religious instruction you may have received, ethnic heritage, influences of your close friends and their parents, and the activities you pursue.

In a classroom discussion, each person is both a learner and a teacher. Listen carefully to the views and experiences of your peers. But you should also be prepared to share your experiences and ideas. By participating actively in this way, you will become a teacher, as well as a student, and you will greatly enrich your learning experience and the learning experiences of others.

As your discussions proceed, the issues of the cases will become clearer and your understanding of the options will be enhanced and refined. The cases have been written to expand your perspectives, to enlarge your knowledge, to grow your understanding, and to deepen your insight into your values and yourself.

You should set aside time to reflect on the particulars of the case after the class discussion. Ask yourself this important question: "What have I learned from this experience that will make me a more responsible person in my daily life as a family member, a student and in other endeavors across an array of experiential realms?"

You may choose to keep a journal of your reflections on the case discussions and also note later experiences that reflect how the lessons learned had an impact on your behavior and actions. These discoveries will allow you to chart the progress of your learning experiences. The more you invest in these discoveries, the richer will be the rewards. Thoughtful and refined reading and examination will lead you to new insights and perspectives.

Remember: learning is not linear. It comes in steps and stages. Some insights arrive as small, discrete revelations; others arrive almost as epiphanies and are equivalent to giant leaps in knowledge and understanding of yourself. You have had experiences wrestling with a problem and then experiencing the "Aha!" moment of a new insight. Give yourself over to these cases, and you will have many more such moments of insight and revelation.

The cases are about choices that people face in life. Exploring these cases will help you determine how values shape your thinking and bring about a more sophisticated understanding of the impact your talents, energies, and personal leadership can have on your life and the lives of those in your community.

Cheating at McDaniel College

Jane Merkley is loving her freshman year of school at McDaniel College in upstate Vermont. She had graduated from Jackson High School in Weston, Virginia. Most students graduating from Jackson did not go on to college, but Jane wanted to be a film or music producer, and McDaniel had very respected theater and music programs. Jane had applied only to McDaniel, and she was thrilled when she got accepted.

Now in her fourth month at school, Jane is facing her first final exams. She is quite confident about her Shakespearean literature and western civilization courses, but she is nervous about Introduction to Calculus. Jane is no math whiz, that is for sure. But the test is a take-home exam, which means that she can take the test at her desired location and pace. However, she is required to complete the test without any assistance from others, and she is instructed not to refer to her class notes or textbook.

It is 11:30 the night before the calculus exam is due, and Jane is in the campus library. The library stays open 24 hours a day throughout the period of final exams. This is good for Jane, as she knows that she might spend most of the night in the library working on the test.

Jane decides to take a break and she walks toward the library's vending machine room. As she rounds a corner, she overhears some students talking about the exam. Jane recognizes the voices as Alap Bheda and Deepinder Sweeta, who are in her calculus class. They are discussing problem number three on the test. Jane had already looked at that problem but had not figured it out.

McDaniel College has a strict honor code that is student enforced. Every student, upon completing any exam, must write and sign the following: "I pledge that I have neither given nor received help on this test, nor am I aware of anyone who has."

Jane suspects that Alap and Deepinder are violating the honor code, and she would be too if she did not report their actions. She thinks about approaching them, but she does not know them very well and she is concerned about how they might react. Jane wonders whether Alap and Deepinder would stop discussing the exam if she approached them or if they would just ignore her.

Jane does not want to be a "tattle-tail" or the kind of person who is into everybody's business. In this case, however, she is concerned that if she writes and signs the honor pledge on her exam, she will be lying about the fact that she is not aware of anyone who may have cheated. Jane takes the honor code very seriously. It is because of the code that she can do a take-home exam. She is pretty sure that she could not pass the exam if it were not for the extra time provided by its being a take-home assignment.

Finally Jane decides to simply ask Alap and Deepinder to stop their collaboration. By doing this, she wonders if she will have fulfilled her responsibilities to adhere to the honor code.

Jane approaches Alap and Deepinder and says, "Hey, I couldn't help overhearing you guys talking about the calculus exam. I'm just reminding you that the professor said that it was an individual test, so we should not be discussing the answers or our ideas with each other. That would be an honor code violation and would be considered cheating."

Alap and Deepinder laugh. Alap responds to Jane, "We know about the honor code and all, but we also believe we should help each other out. Deepinder had a question about the language in the question, and I was helping him figure it out. It's not cheating; it's helping."

Deepinder adds, "For us, our obligation is to our community more than anything else. Here at McDaniel, we also signed a pledge stating that we would honor our community and build relationships of respect, trust and support. That is the other code we honor too."

Jane doesn't know what to say. She simply responds, "I see."

Should Jane accept their responses, even though she had definitely heard them talking about formulas and not just the language of the question? Also, Alap and Deepinder appeared to be sharing notes, doing calculations, and comparing their work. While they had a good point about the community pledge that they had all signed at freshman orientation, the question remained: Which is the more important pledge in this instance, honor or community?

Rick Reynolds Needs a Signature

Rick Reynolds sits at the desk in his bedroom staring at a note from Ms. Nancy Crawford, his sophomore math teacher. Ms. Crawford sent the note home with Rick with instructions for him to show the note to his father, get his father's signature on the note, and return it to her the following day.

Rick's father is a cantankerous man. Rick knows that his dad, when he reads the note, will in all likelihood prohibit Rick from trying out for the basketball team.

Earlier that afternoon, Ms. Crawford had caught three students copying Rick's answers to a pop quiz. Rick did not feel comfortable allowing his friends to copy his answers, but he was new to the school and it was not easy for him to say no.

Rick is 16 years old and a sophomore at Lincoln High School. Rick and his father had moved recently to Lincoln, Nebraska, from Kentucky, after his mother's death. Rick's father had accepted a job as a cost accountant at a local manufacturing company.

The move to Lincoln had not been an easy one for Rick. To make matters worse, he had been cut from the school's JV football team only a week after he had tried out. Rick found it difficult fitting in at Lincoln High, but he took some solace in the hope that he would make the basketball team and be given an opportunity to make new friends on the court.

Rick's father is a strict disciplinarian who believes in putting academics before sports. John Reynolds has always held Rick accountable for his actions. While Rick knows that he could explain to his dad what really happened today at school, he also knows that Mr. Reynolds would in all likelihood contact Ms. Crawford as well as the other guys' parents, which would cause Rick great embarrassment. However, if Rick accepts the blame, his father will prevent him from trying out for the basketball team.

Weighing his options, Rick is now thinking that he might forge his father's signature on the note. He reasons that Ms. Crawford likely would not know the difference. She has never seen his father's handwriting. Rick remembers that friends back in Kentucky had successfully pulled off the same ruse.

Rick asks himself, What's the harm? After all, he had learned his lesson. He would never again allow a classmate to copy his work. And a little white lie, such as this, far outweighs the risk of embarrassment, his father's anger, and further isolation from his peers at school.

Rick thought that, after all, it was his father who had forced him to move away from his old friends. Rick would simply be doing what he needed to do to survive in his new school. Furthermore, he was the true victim here. It was not his fault that the other students were cheating off his exam.

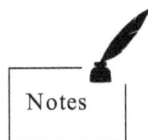

Debra Gotfried and Ritalin

Debra Gotfried is on the stage at the Medford High School graduation going over the notes for her speech. She is the valedictorian of her class, and tradition dictates that she has the honor of addressing her peers and teachers with a valedictory speech.

Debra is both proud and humbled to be the valedictorian, especially since only four years ago she had been just a slightly above average student. As the other honored guests at today's event are speaking, Debra reflects on her high school experiences. Her thoughts drift back to an episode during the second semester of her freshman year.

Debra had always been a procrastinator. She was never motivated to write a paper, study for a test, or work on an assigned project until the deadline loomed close. During her freshman year in high school, Debra was working on a team social studies project with three classmates, including Sarah, her best friend's girlfriend. They had been assigned the task of conceptualizing a make-believe country that included a governmental system, money, history, geography and cultural references. It was an interesting assignment to all four students, but Debra lacked the motivation and focus to commit fully to the project.

One week before the project was due, the team had a meeting to assess progress and assign final tasks to complete the assignment. Sarah, sensing a lack of motivation in Debra, offered her a pill to help her focus her attention. "It's Ritalin," Sarah said. "I take it for my attention deficit disorder (ADD) and it helps me get back to normal. If I don't take it, I can barely watch a YouTube video without getting distracted. It might help you. Maybe you have ADD like me."

While Debra did not really think that she had ADD, she knew that she was having a difficult time focusing on the project. Debra was not the kind of person who experiments with drugs, and she had never taken Ritalin. But, from the way Sarah described it, Ritalin did not seem to be any worse than those caffeine energy drinks like Red Bull that were available at any grocery or convenience store.

Debra found that the Ritalin acted on her exactly as Sarah had described. She discovered that she could sit for several hours at a time and write papers, conduct research, or do assigned reading on any topic, no matter how boring it seemed to her.

Ultimately, Debra asked Sarah for more of the pills. Eventually, she convinced a doctor to write her a prescription.

During the coming weeks, Debra's grades improved and she no longer turned in late or incomplete assignments. While there were a few side effects, like weight loss, bouts of anxiety, and insomnia, Debra came to enjoy the increased productivity and the feeling of accomplishment too much to stop taking the Ritalin.

That was almost four years ago. Debra has not gone a day without Ritalin since.

As Debra now looks out into the audience, she sees Brett Jones, a star running back. Brett had been kicked off the football team last fall, right before the last game of the year, for using performance enhancers. Football is big in Medford, Oregon. Brett has been offered a scholarship to Washington State, a scholarship that is now in jeopardy because of Brett's dismissal from the team. Without financial aid, it is doubtful that Brett would be able to attend college.

Brett had not been "doping" with steroids or anything hardcore. Debra had heard that Brett had simply been drinking enhanced protein shakes for muscle growth and energy. But school administrators determined that this gave Brett an unfair advantage over the rest of the team and, potentially, the team's opponents. Students and people in the community spoke openly about whether Brett would have been such a superior athlete if he had not taken the protein shakes.

Debra thinks that it will be a shame if Brett does not receive his scholarship, but now she remembers that she had agreed with the decision to kick him off the team. Performance enhancing substances are not fair in sports, and they can be dangerous.

Now Debra is wondering whether her Ritalin use might be considered a performance enhancer. Indeed, would she even be sitting here on the stage at graduation about to give the valedictory speech had she not started taking Ritalin? Debra wonders if she is an addict and whether she will still need Ritalin in college—and for the rest of her life.

Molly Graham's Situation

Sixteen year old Molly Graham is a student at Sunrise Hills High School. She has lived her entire life in Minneapolis. Molly has attended school with the same group of students since kindergarten, which makes her current situation all the more difficult.

Two weeks ago Molly discovered that she is pregnant. She had not been feeling well, especially in the mornings. When she missed her period, Molly purchased an at-home pregnancy test and then confirmed the result with her family physician.

Her family, after expressing initial shock, has taken the news pretty well. In fact, they are very supportive. They want her to keep the baby, and they promise to help out in any way they can. Molly is not surprised by this, as her parents are quite conservative and they oppose abortion. Molly knows that consideration of an abortion will never be an option for them.

Molly's boyfriend, Cody Simpson, is another story entirely. She and Cody have not argued or broken up over the pregnancy. He is simply shocked, as is Molly, that "the problem," as Cody calls it, could even have occurred, given that she was on birth control.

Molly does not know whether she wants to keep the baby. One consideration, perhaps paramount among the many issues involved, has to do with her education and career plans. Molly has long dreamed of becoming a nurse. In fact, she is taking some advanced chemistry classes at Sunrise Hills High to better prepare for nursing school. She has also applied and is expected to get selected for a very competitive program that permits a small number of qualified students at Sunrise Hills High to enroll in anatomy classes at the University of Minnesota.

Molly knows that her pregnancy will change her plans significantly, but not because she cannot manage both pregnancy and school work. School board policy dictates that pregnant students cannot remain in standard high school. They must transfer to an alternative school or leave school altogether and return after the baby's birth. Alternative schools were established for students who need a greater degree of discipline, or for those whose behavior has led to their being expelled from the standard high schools in the system.

Molly cannot imagine herself pregnant and in an alternative school. And as she is now a junior, Molly knows that with the unfortunate timing of the pregnancy, she will likely graduate from the alternative school. This will be difficult to explain on her college applications. If, on the other hand, Molly were to quit school to have the baby, she worries that she might not go back to school. What kind of life can she expect without a high school diploma? How can she support the child? Quitting school will certainly mean that she would not become a nurse in the near future.

Cody, Molly's boyfriend, is a star varsity soccer player at Sunrise Hills High. He is also a junior with plans for college. He expects to get a scholarship to play soccer at the University of California Los Angeles (UCLA). In addition to being a sports star, Cody is also good at math. And he enjoys building models of cars and airplanes. He is thinking about studying engineering.

Cody met Molly when they were in the third grade, after he transferred to Minneapolis from Sunnydale, CA. Cody's father had accepted a position at a local General Mills plant. In the seventh grade, Cody had finally asked Molly out to attend the middle school year-end dance. They have been dating ever since.

Cody and Molly have been sexually active for over a year. Both sets of parents are aware of this and Molly is on birth control pills.

While Cody had not considered life without Molly, he is not ready to propose marriage yet. But now that she is pregnant, he wonders what he should do. If they decide to keep the baby, Molly will go to the alternative school, and they likely will be able to see each other only on the weekends. This will certainly place an added strain on the relationship, especially since Cody is often out of town on weekends due to soccer games.

Cody knows that there will probably be pressure on him and Molly to marry, but he does not think that he is ready for fatherhood or marriage. If he and Molly give the baby up for adoption, they will not feel obliged to marry at this time. And if they decide to abort the fetus, they could both stay at Sunrise Hills High, but this would disappoint her parents deeply.

Molly knows that her life will change forever if she decides to keep the baby. Molly also knows that even if she gives the baby up for adoption, she might have to postpone her dream of going to nursing school immediately after high school.

Molly worries about what will become of her and Cody's relationship. If she does choose to carry the baby to term, she will be transferred to the alternative high school across town. That could lead to Cody finding someone else to date.

Molly does not know what to do. She watches from her car as her friends enter Sunrise High for another day of school. Molly wonders how many of them will actually care that she is pregnant.

How great it would be if Molly actually had the option of remaining at Sunrise High to finish her studies and graduate!

Angie's Book

Rachel Gifford is sitting in her AP American History class when she gets a text message from her good friend Mark. It reads, "They sent Angie's book home. Everyone's parents have the whole book. Nice knowing you all." Rachel is frozen with fear. She had put a lot of personal stuff in the book without even really considering the possibility that others might read it.

Angie Wilson is leaving Summer Heights High School in upstate New York and moving to Jacksonville, Florida, because her father has received a promotion at his company. It is her junior year. Angie has made a lot of friends at Summer Heights, and she wants to have something to remind her of them and the fun they have had together.

Angie had purchased a spiral notebook and had written questions at the top of each page. She started out with easy questions, such as ones about age, favorite colors, food, and other innocuous personal information. However, after about fifteen of these kinds of questions, Angie had gotten more personal: "How many boyfriends or girlfriends have you had? How many people have you kissed? Have you ever had sex? With whom?" The questions toward the end of Angie's survey were really risky because the answers, she knew, could get people in trouble if they became known. However, Angie did not plan on sharing the book with anyone but her closest friends. Her questions asked about drug and alcohol experimentation and use, such as: "What drugs have you tried? How many times have you gotten drunk?"

After Angie had filled the notebook with questions, she gave it to her best friend Tiffany Yoder to begin the process of answering the questions. After Tiffany had finished her responses, she then passed the notebook along to another of Angie's friends, who took the next row down and answered the questions on each page. This process continued with others until, in less than a week, all the rows had been filled, and Angie's notebook was complete.

Rachel's answers were near the top of the pages because Angie was one of her best friends. Rachel had been given the book before most of the other people.

Rachel had been pretty shocked by how personal some of the questions were. But her friend Angie knew all of the information anyway, so what could be the harm, she thought. Plus, it would be cool to see everyone else's responses when the book was complete. Rachel had exaggerated a bit in her answers to some of the questions. She knew others were going to see her responses, and she did not want to seem uncool. Rachel also knew that other people had exaggerated their answers too. She and her friends had never dreamed that their parents would see the book!

When Mr. Atkins confiscated the book in class, Rachel thought that he would just throw it away. This is what he had always done with notes he had confiscated from students in class. But that is not what happened this time, and now Rachel simply does not know what to do.

Rachel is justifiably fearful of her mother's response. Rachel had shared a lot with her mom through the years, as they have grown very close since her father died. But Rachel's answers to the questions that are in the book are a different story altogether. Rachel knows that her mom will be hurt if she believes all of Rachel's answers are true and that Rachel had not shared this information already.

Gina Gifford, Rachel's mom, has just opened the package that the mailroom delivery boy had dropped off at her desk. She is a paralegal at the law offices of Anderson and Smith. The package is from her eldest daughter's high school. The school had never sent anything to her at work before, so she is truly concerned. Inside the package Mrs. Gifford finds a copy of a spiral notebook that has questions on every page and different students' answers to those questions in rows underneath. Her daughter's answers are highlighted. Mrs. Gifford is shocked at what she reads.

While the other students' names are blacked out, their answers are not. The students' answers to the questions range from the funny and benign to the personal and scandalous. Her daughter Rachel has provided answers that include information about which Mrs. Gifford was unaware, personal information that her daughter had apparently felt comfortable sharing with her classmates.

The notebook came with a note from Ms. Anne Khore, the principal of Summer Heights High School. The note says: "This notebook has been confiscated in class. Its contents are such that we feel the participating students' parents should be apprised of the situation."

Mrs. Gifford does not know what to do with the book. Should she tell Rachel about it? Should she ask Rachel to explain some of the more disturbing information in order to determine whether or not she was telling the

truth in the book? Should she be upset with
the school for violating her daughter's privacy?

Mark Pittman's Party

Mark Pittman was thrilled and a little scared when he got the news from the recruiter. He was to be sworn into the U.S. Army one hour after graduating from high school. Mark knows that "going Army" is the right choice for him, and his parents support his choice too. Mark needed their consent to enlist, as he is only 17 years old.

Mark plans to go to college on the GI bill after his time in the Army. He is aware, however, that it is a dangerous time to enter the military, what with wars ongoing in the Middle East. There is a chance he might not make it home, especially since he will have a low rank and likely be involved in front line activities.

Mark had already spoken with his parents about hosting a party to celebrate his graduation and to say goodbye to his friends prior to leaving for boot camp.

Mark is getting a little stressed when he thinks about the party. He decides that it would be good to have some beer on hand to lighten the mood. Mark and his buddies are not big drinkers, and he does not see a problem with having a beer or two, despite the fact that he is only 17. He needs his parents to buy the beer for him and his friends. He has already begun building his case to take to his parents to convince them to provide alcohol for his party.

Prior to alcohol prohibition in 1919, most states did not have a minimum drinking age. After the repeal of prohibition in 1933, states set the drinking age at the so-called "age of majority," which at the time was 21. In 1971, the 26th Amendment, which lowered the age at which U.S. citizens can vote to 18, was passed. This amendment was mostly in response to concerns that men could be conscripted into the military at the age of 18 but could not vote in elections that might have an impact on the course of war. With the passage of the 26th Amendment, most states lowered their age of majority and, effectively, the minimum drinking age.

In 1984, Congress passed the National Minimum Drinking Age Act. This legislation raised the federal minimum drinking age back to 21 to address the problem of teenage drunk driving accidents. It was a federal law, but states were given the choice to "opt out" and make their own determinations regarding the age of majority as it related to drinking. Should a state choose to opt out, however, by federal mandate it would lose ten percent of its annual federal highway appropriation. In July, 1988, Wyoming became the last state to opt into the law, which raised the state's legal drinking age from 19 to 21. News reports at the time claimed that Wyoming would have lost $8.2 million in federal funding every year if it had not opted in. Several state legislators called it "federal blackmail." Mark's state of South Carolina had raised the minimum drinking age to 21 in 1986.

More recent debates about the appropriate drinking age centered on a new problem: binge drinking. Critics argued that by setting the legal drinking age at 21, the government was, in effect, forcing drinking underground. Teenagers then consumed larger quantities of alcohol and in more reckless ways. Underage drinkers tend to drink too much, too quickly, and they become ill as a result. They are often too frightened to call for help because they know they have acted illegally.

A 2006 study by the U.S. Department of Health and Human Services found that at any given time approximately twenty-eight percent of teens between 12 and 20 years old had consumed alcohol during the previous month. Fully nineteen percent of such incidences were considered "binge" drinking. A consortium of college presidents submitted a proposal to the government to remove the link to highway funds and allow states to decide the minimum age for legal drinking. The group proposed that if a state were to set a legal age for drinking lower than 21, it would establish an alcohol education program and issue licenses to drink to those who have completed the course.

Proponents of the original law had proof that the number of drunk driving fatalities had declined since the enactment in 1984 of the National Minimum Drinking Age Act, and they argued for greater enforcement. They also argued that drinking at a young age is simply unhealthy and should be illegal to prevent abuse.

There were also concerns about young people drinking where adjacent states had different legal minimum drinking ages. Idaho raised its minimum drinking age from 19 to 21 in 1987. Washington's minimum drinking age had been 21 since the repeal of prohibition. There is a ten-mile stretch of highway between Idaho and the state of Washington that, prior to 1987, was infamous for the many drunk driving accidents that occurred there. That route connected Washington State University (WSU) in Pullman to the University of Idaho in Moscow. WSU students would travel to Idaho to buy and drink alcohol in bars and at parties and then drive back to Pullman. Since the route was not that long or complex, students thought they could make the trip without being caught or involved in an accident. They were often mistaken, sometimes with tragic consequences.

Mark is sitting in his bedroom. Many thoughts regarding his problem are floating around in his head. He wonders about the discrepancy of being able to choose to serve his country and go to war but not being able to have a drink. He also needs to consider his parents' obligations and responsibilities, both legal and personal, to his friends for their safety, and the rights of his friends' parents to know about the presence of alcohol at the party. Just then the door opens and Mark's mother comes into the room. "Mark, have you given any more thought to your party?"

A Second Chance for John O'Brien

It was a Saturday afternoon around 5:00 p.m. when Dennis Roberts, a teacher at the Buckley School, decided to drop by and see what the guys in The Wavy Gravies band were doing. Upon entering the rehearsal room in the Performing Arts Center, Mr. Roberts found John O'Brien, C.J. Carmichael, Rick Sims, and Bob Conner standing together near an open window. Roberts saw that Rick was holding a small glass pipe. He knew immediately that Rick, and perhaps others in the group, had been smoking marijuana.

Following protocol, Dennis Roberts immediately notified John Holtz, the Dean of Students, and explained what he had observed. Mr. Roberts was then instructed to bring the boys to the Dean's office immediately while Dean Holtz notified Dr. William Cox, the headmaster.

Upon hearing the details of the episode, Dr. Cox grasped the severity of the situation. He realized that he would not, indeed could not allow a violation of this severity to go unpunished.

Drugs, drug paraphernalia, and alcohol are strictly forbidden at The Buckley School. It is stated policy that the possession, use, or presence of any illicit or otherwise prohibited substance will result in immediate expulsion. In the past, Headmaster Cox's decisions to expel students in similar situations were thought to be appropriately decisive.

John's case, however, is in the headmaster's opinion marked by considerable extenuating circumstances. O'Brien was raised by his grandmother in Camden, New Jersey. He is an only child. His father is in prison and his mother is dead. At The Buckley School John has an exemplary record and is a 4.0 student and a varsity all-star athlete, excelling in soccer, basketball and baseball since his freshman year. In addition to his athletic and academic achievements, John is a talented musician who plays trumpet in the school's jazz band and lead guitar in his student rock band.

John O'Brien had come to The Buckley School on scholarship. Even though O'Brien is still a junior, the headmaster knows that it is likely that John will graduate at the top of his class and gain a full scholarship to a college or university. He has never before been involved in a disciplinary situation at Buckley. O'Brien is the embodiment of what a Buckley boy should be, and Dr. Cox feels he is lucky to have him in the student body.

The Buckley School, located near Pittsfield, in western Massachusetts, is a private, co-ed boarding school that was founded as an all-boys academy in 1867 by the iron magnate Zacharias Buckley. The son of a Methodist minister who set an example of stewardship for the boys, Mr. Buckley bestowed his fortune and name on a school whose mission would be to produce "God-fearing boys of character" who would go on to become leaders in society. Through the years The Buckley School had continued to adhere to its traditional values, with its administrators and faculty always taking great pride in the school's acclaimed Buckley Honor Code.

Dennis Roberts is typical of many boarding school teachers: a young, multi-talented individual who was hired by The Buckley School to teach, coach athletes, and serve as a dormitory master. Mr. Roberts had come to Buckley three years before after graduating *magna cum laude* from Bowdoin College. Since joining the faculty at Buckley, Dennis has won the respect of his fellow teachers and the admiration of the school's 450 students.

On weekends Mr. Roberts spends time with the students playing soccer, basketball or improvising with members of the jazz band. He plays drums and alto sax. Because of his relative youth and the fact that he is a patient teacher, Mr. Roberts relates well to Buckley's student body.

John O'Brien, though quite different in character and personality from the other three boys, had become friends with Rick, Bob, and C.J. when the four had joined the campus jazz band. Later they had formed their own rock group, which they named The Wavy Gravies. Rick, Bob, and C.J. are "nice kids," but most teachers suspected that they were often "up to something." John, disciplined student that he is, rarely socializes with the other members of the group because of his demanding academic and athletic schedules.

Marijuana use by Buckley students is punishable by expulsion. Moreover, school policy dictates that the possession and/or use of prohibited substances of any kind, including alcohol, must be reported by teachers and students alike. The reality, however, is that John, like most students, often ignores his peers' questionable behavior, even though the Honor Code is explicit in stating in sentence three, paragraph four that even "those in the presence of activities violating Buckley standards will face the same punishment as those engaged in the prohibited activities themselves."

After turning the students in, Mr. Roberts is quick to come to John's defense and requests of the headmaster special consideration. He pleads that John was simply "in the wrong place at the wrong time." In addition, several other teachers, including Mr. Phil Koch, John's baseball coach, rise to John's defense.

John's peers, including Rick, Bob, and C.J., who have already been informed that they will be dismissed, also vouch for John, claiming that he has never used marijuana in their presence.

However, Mr. Holtz, the Dean of Students, is less sympathetic. While he agrees with his colleagues that John is one of Buckley's best students, he contends that the rules should apply equally to everyone.

The headmaster's decision on John's fate will have to be made by the morning. Dr. Cox knows that it will not be an easy one. If he does not punish John O'Brien with expulsion, he will appear to be favoring one student above the others, while also turning his back on the honor code that has been so assiduously guarded for nearly 150 years. However, John is clearly a great student with a promising future, a young man whose dreams of a full scholarship to college likely will go unfulfilled if he were to be expelled from Buckley.

The Whiterock Football Team

Trent Miller, a junior defensive back for the football team at Whiterock University in central Arizona, is dining with his parents at the Oak Barrel Steakhouse. The Whiterock football team had just defeated North Central State 10-7 on a last minute touchdown scored by their star senior, all-conference running back José Gonzalez, known to his schoolmates as Go-Go.

While eating, Trent sees Go-Go and his parents and sister enter the restaurant and be seated by the hostess. Trent notices that the hostess offers the Gonzalez family a choice table at the front of the restaurant, which Go-Go politely declines. The family takes instead a table in the back of the restaurant near the kitchen. Go-Go has not seen Trent and his parents, who are seated in a crowded section at the center of the restaurant.

During the meal, Trent sees Go-Go drinking a Sierra-Nevada, a popular west coast beer. This is a violation of a rule that the Whiterock University football team members had established prior to the season that stated: "No player, even if he is over 21, may drink alcohol during football season on any occasion." The rule is enforced by what Head Coach Gary Mercer called "the honor and buddy system." This means that a player is accountable for his own behavior and the behavior of his teammates. Team members are expected to report violations of team rules to Coach Mercer within 24 hours of their having been observed.

Whiterock University is a small state school located in central Arizona. Whiterock has 6,517 students, most of whom claim in-state residency. Whiterock University is well known for its liberal arts education and strong philosophy and arts programs. Whiterock has been a member of the Sun Belt Alliance Conference (SBAC) for the past 20 years. The SBAC is composed of 14 member colleges and universities, all of which are located in the Southwest or along the Pacific coast. The SBAC is a Division II conference, covering eight male athletic programs and nine female athletic programs at each of its member institutions.

Whiterock had fielded a sub-par football team for most of its history. However, the school had made a widely publicized turnaround under the leadership of Head Coach Gary Mercer. Coach Mercer joined

Whiterock four years ago. In his second season, he led the school to a 10-1 record, the best finish in school history. Last year, Whiterock was undefeated entering the final game of the season, but they fell short in that game, losing 28-21 to eventual conference champion East Texas State.

One of the reasons Whiterock University's football team lost the game was that its star running back, Go-Go Gonzalez, was sidelined by an injury he sustained on the first play of the game. The loss ended Whiterock's perfect season, its SBAC conference championship run, and any playoff hopes. If the team had won the game, Whiterock, as the conference champion, would have competed in the national playoffs.

This year's Whiterock University football team has won ten games and is undefeated. On the next weekend, Whiterock plays its final regular season game against Western Polytechnic Institute (West Tech), a state school in neighboring New Mexico. The winner will be crowned SBAC conference champion and receive an automatic bid to the football national championship series playoffs.

One of the major changes Coach Mercer had initiated during his tenure as coach at Whiterock was the establishment of a set of rules for team members. Coach Mercer decided to have a player advisory council to help create, with input from the coaching staff, a first draft of team objectives, goals, and rules. Before finalization, all team members reviewed the list of objectives, goals, and rules and either agreed or suggested changes to the initial draft. This interactive approach was designed to promote team unity and a sense of accountability by all members of the team. The player advisory council consisted of the team's co-captains, which were Trent and Go-Go, and one additional representative from each class.

During the rule setting meeting, Coach Mercer stressed the importance of team spirit and frequently spoke of team members as being brothers, responsible for each other on and off the field. The meeting lasted for over four hours as coaches and players deliberated the issue of a "dry season." Prior team rules had included a three drink maximum for legal-aged team members on Saturday nights only. Coach Mercer and some current players attributed Whiterock's historical sub-par football team performance, in part, to team rules that were too lenient.

Members of the player advisory council agreed that alcohol consumption could be detrimental to team members' health and athletic performance, so they came out in favor of a "dry season." A dry season prohibited any team member, regardless of age, from consuming any type of alcohol during the season, regardless of the occasion.

At the conclusion of the rule setting meeting, Coach Mercer, the player advisory council, and the rest of the team had congregated in the film meeting room to finalize the team's list of objectives, goals, and rules. To clarify the "dry season" rule, a player advisory council member had asked the entire team whether it was okay to drink a beer with your family after a game. The question was met with a resounding "NO" that echoed through the film room. Coach Mercer impressed upon the players that rules are rules, not suggestions for behavior, and he said that no exceptions are to be made. Any violator of a rule would be subject to immediate suspension, regardless of who he is.

Coach Mercer's final statement at the meeting was, "Team members will adhere to the rules, knowing the negative impact of being suspended and its effect on the team's overall success." A week after the rules were made, the player advisory council held a team meeting to review each rule again and to provide a hard copy of the rules to each member of the Whiterock football team. To further emphasize the importance of the rules to the team, Coach Mercer hung large posters of the rules in both the weight room and locker room.

During the sixth week of this football season, a violation of team rules had occurred. After an amazing 24-21 overtime win against Bluffington College, Leighton Mobley, a sophomore defensive end, was observed by Go-Go Gonzalez drinking a beer at a fraternity party. Leighton had pleaded with Go-Go not to inform Coach Mercer about the rule violation, contending that it was only one celebratory beer after the big win against Bluffington. Go-Go had told Leighton that each team member must be accountable for his own actions as well as the actions of others. He emphasized that if he did not report the drinking violation to Coach Mercer within 24 hours, he would be in direct violation of the team's honor system. Go-Go reported the incident to Coach Mercer, and Leighton was suspended from the team for two weeks.

Trent mentions to his father the situation that he is observing at the restaurant and asks what he should do. Trent's father answers, "Son, the team's policy sounds strict, but it is the team's policy. You are facing a dilemma, but it is your dilemma. Think through the situation carefully and I am sure you will make the right decision."

An Intern's Dilemma

Suzanne Patel had looked forward to the talent show all week. On the day of the show, she could barely focus on the work that she had to do for her internship.

Baath & Thomas, her summer employer in Chicago and one of the "Big Three" accounting firms, has one of the best internship programs in the country. To keep their interns happy and to provide social opportunities for them outside of work, Baath & Thomas hosts a variety of events throughout the summer to allow the interns to network and mingle with one another.

The firm had been advertising the talent show as "the highlight of the internship experience at Baath & Thomas." The firm's full-time staff was pushing the excitement of the talent show and mandated that in order for an intern to attend the event, he or she must participate in the show. This year's event was scheduled be held in the banquet room of one of Chicago's nicest hotels, The Grand Millennium Hotel, and would be lavishly catered.

Suzanne works at a client site, located a few miles outside the city. As her family lives in the nearby suburbs, Suzanne had decided to save money and move in with her parents for the summer. When she started the internship, Suzanne took the train to work from her parents' home because it stopped near the client site on the way into the city. After work, Suzanne would sometimes go into the city and see some of her friends; other times she would simply take the train straight home. Toward the middle of the summer, Suzanne grew tired of the train and its somewhat inconvenient schedule and opted on most days to drive back and forth to work.

On the morning of the talent show, which would take her into the city that evening, Suzanne pondered how best to get to work. She was told at the start of the internship that she could expense transportation costs to and from the social events for interns. If she rode the train to work, she could ride into the city and then back home later that night. The train was inexpensive, costing fewer than five dollars in transportation expenses. However, being familiar with the hotel where the event was being held, Suzanne knew that, if she were to drive, she could valet her car at the hotel. This, however, would cost more than forty dollars, without gratuity.

As Suzanne was getting ready to leave home, she remembered that some of her fellow interns did not have train-accessible client sites, and many would be driving into the city and valet parking their cars at the hotel. While it was tempting to drive in, Suzanne also wanted to take advantage of the open bar and did not want to drink and drive. She decided to take the train.

On the Monday after the party, Suzanne leaves the client site after lunch to go into the city to deliver some client work to the Baath & Thomas office. While she is there, she decides to fill out her expense report and drop it off in the accounting office.

Suzanne bumps into a few of her fellow interns, who also happen to be running errands for their respective teams. She sits with them in the break room as she fills out her report, listing her train travel expenses. Tony Hughes, another intern and a friend who happens to be glancing over her shoulder, remarks, "Suzanne, what are you doing?! You live in the suburbs. Most of us put down that we drove in, and we don't even live as far out as you do. You can make like forty bucks by expensing the parking fee. And it's under fifty dollars, so you don't even need a receipt. One of my team members said that it was legitimate and no one ever checks. Besides, the expense reports are processed in Dallas or somewhere else far from here. No one will ever know."

Voting for the First Time

This is Brad Harrison's first time voting. He turned 18 in August. As he waits in the line to go into the voting booth, he is reading a summary of the initiatives on the ballot. He begins thinking that he should have read this a little earlier than right before voting. He has been paying attention to who is running for President, and he knows his decision on that vote. As he is reading the other items on the ballot, one initiative catches his eye: legalizing and taxing the sale and consumption of small quantities of marijuana for recreational purposes.

Brad has never tried marijuana. He has friends who have, and they have not turned into "huge stoners" or anything like that. Then again, Brad has chosen not to try it because he believes it may be a dangerous drug, and he is worried about the risks. The fact that the state is considering legalizing it for recreational purposes has made Brad question the validity of these concerns and also whether legalizing marijuana would be good for society. This vote seems very important, and he wants to take it seriously.

Marijuana use is legal in some countries, including China, Cambodia, the Netherlands, and Romania. In most countries, however, marijuana is considered an illegal substance, and its use is often treated with the same severe penalties as illegal narcotics, though it is not classified as a narcotic.

In the United States, marijuana became illegal in 1937 along with narcotic drugs, such as heroin and cocaine. Marijuana generally is classified as a Schedule I drug, which means it has no medical use. Several states, including Washington State where Brad lives, have changed its classification to Schedule II, which allows for some potential medical use.

In the early 19th century and before, marijuana (or hemp) had been used primarily in medicines and textiles, but it was much less potent than today's crops. Its recreational use grew in the 19th century and, as a result, it was often classified with other narcotics.

Brad recalls seeing statistics that reported that over forty percent of students have tried marijuana by the time they are seniors in high school, and over twenty percent have used the drug at least once during the past few months. He also remembers reading that students who participate in sports or other extracurricular activities are less likely to use marijuana.

Students most likely to use drugs have grades in the B and C range or lower, frequently come from single-parent households, and are more likely to hold after school jobs. Among American adults, eighteen percent of those between the ages of 18 and 34, thirty-six percent between the ages of 35 and 49, and twenty-eight percent of those over age 50 report that they have used marijuana.

Brad's state of Washington is currently debating the issue of allowing the sale and possession of marijuana for up to one ounce for recreational use. Marijuana would be sold only in state liquor stores to persons over the age of 21 years and would have a tax of $50 per ounce. The revenue from the tax has not yet been earmarked, but discussion has centered on spending the money on substance abuse prevention or arts and music programs in public schools. Advocates of the law estimate that the state could gain up to $300 million annually from the tax.

Washington already has a legal marijuana law for medicinal purposes. This law requires a doctor's prescription to purchase and possess marijuana and does not have a tax on it. The new legislation will allow anyone 21 years or older to purchase a small quantity of marijuana, but they would have to pay the tax.

The creators of the proposed law on the ballot suggest that marijuana could be sold and regulated with a "sin tax" attached, just as there is with the sale of tobacco and alcohol. A sin tax is a tax that is levied above and beyond the sales tax on products that have the potential to cause harm and strain the public healthcare system. In the case of cigarettes, Washington State adds a $2.25 tax to every pack sold, and the money collected is devoted to programs to help people quit smoking. The tax rests on the assumption that cigarettes are hazardous to one's health.

Brad worries about the health risks of using marijuana. He is no expert on the subject, and medical experts themselves are conflicted on the topic of the risks of marijuana use. But Brad knows how lethargic and silly his friends become sometimes when they are smoking marijuana, and he wonders whether it really is as harmless as some say.

Brad remembers that just last year he had overheard a teacher, Mr. Jim Harris, talking to Brad's friend Steve about some changes he had observed in Steve's school work. Mr. Harris suspected that marijuana use might be responsible for the decline in the quality of the assignments that Steve was turning in. Mr. Harris was pretty sanguine about it, but he did say that Steve's performance had been slipping and that he felt compelled to point out that different people have different tolerance levels for chemicals in the body.

The argument for additional tax money makes sense to Brad, since he has seen some useful programs at his school shut down for lack of money. He used to love playing the drums in music class, but the school had cancelled the class last year due to funding cuts. Brad was facing a tough decision as he approached the voting booth.

A Tough Call

When Katherine McCoy slid into a corner booth at the Harrisburg McDonald's to have her morning coffee and donut, she was feeling stressed. As reported in the copy of the Harrisburg *Patriot-News* that Katherine now had open before her, today she and her colleagues in the Pennsylvania State Legislature would vote on a much-debated bill to ban cell phone use while driving. Katherine knew the vote would be extremely close. She had, in fact, been the object of energetic lobbying over the past few weeks by advocates from both sides of the issue.

At home, Katherine and her husband Joe had gotten into some heated discussions over the matter. As a real estate agent, Joe was opposed to the ban. "It will severely affect my ability to do business, Kat. If I can't take calls from potential clients while I'm on the road, I'll lose a lot of business! You know we can't afford to lose any income, not with Chrissy going off to college next year!"

The thought of their daughter Chrissy making those long drives to and from the university terrified Katherine. She had heard and read the horror stories about teenagers who were killed because they were texting while driving. And from floor debates in the legislature, she knew that statistics indicated that distracted drivers were causing up to sixteen percent of all traffic fatalities. She also knew that research showed that cell phone use while driving causes distraction levels equivalent to a blood alcohol level of 0.08%, which is the legal definition of driving while intoxicated.

Katherine understood her husband's point, but she did not want to play a legislative role in allowing motorists, her daughter included, to text while driving, thereby creating new hazards on the roads.

Thirty states and the District of Columbia have banned texting while driving. Eleven of the laws had been passed within the past year. Some states, such as Maine and New Hampshire, treat cell phone use and texting as part of the larger distracted driving issue. In other states, such as Utah, cell phone use while driving is considered an offense only if a driver is also committing some other moving violation.

Some people assert that the simple solution would be to include an age requirement: "Let adults use cell phones while driving, not teens. We know how to drive responsibly."

Katherine's younger daughter Mara is another story altogether. It is as if Mara is addicted to her cell phone. She is always texting and is constantly chatting away with one or another of her friends. Katherine is pretty sure that it will take more than a piece of legislation to keep Mara off her phone when she begins driving: "Mom, they pass laws on speeding but no one obeys them. People speed until they see a police car, then they slow down. What makes you think that a stupid law banning cell phones will be any different? People are just gonna do what they want!"

Katherine takes another sip of her coffee and wonders whether Mara might be right. Is there something fundamentally wrong with the way policymakers are addressing this issue?

As she finishes her coffee, she recalls the note that Joe had left on top of her briefcase this morning. It said, "I know you'll make the right decision today."

But as Katherine walks out of the McDonald's, a mere 20 minutes before the start of what promises to be a very heated deliberation in the legislature, she is no closer to knowing what that "right decision" should be.

T & T Landscaping

Tyler Taylor watches the tail lights of Chip Green's blue 2002 Ford Ranger disappear down the hill in front of the T&T Landscaping office in Independence, Missouri. Chip, a team supervisor for T&T, had just asked Tyler for a $480 loan in order to avoid the repossession of his wife's 2009 Toyota 4Runner the following afternoon. Tyler told Chip he needed to think about the request overnight and would give him an answer in the morning. It is now 9:15 p.m. as Tyler stands on the porch in front of his office wondering how to handle the situation.

Tyler founded T&T Landscaping in the spring of 2007, after graduating from Kansas State University with a degree in horticulture and a minor in business. T&T specializes in landscaping and residential and retail lawn care. When Tyler established T&T Landscaping, he did not anticipate that so much of his time and energy would be spent dealing with employees and employee-related problems.

At age 24, Tyler now has people working for him who are more than twice his age, and they depend on him for more than a paycheck. Though Tyler is young and single, employees turn to him when they are facing family issues and other important problems. He is pleased that his employees respect him, but the inescapable pressure of running his business, coupled with the challenges of dealing with his employees, weigh on him like a constant numbing hum. The pressure is there when he goes to sleep at night, and it is there when he awakes in the morning.

Chip Green was one of T&T's first employees. He was also Tyler's first pick for team supervisor when he restructured the business into two landscaping and lawn care teams. The company now has five teams, and Chip's team consistently outperforms the other four teams. Chip is 43 years old, has his General Education Diploma, and is married with two teenage daughters. His wife Mary Kay works as a clerk at T. J. Maxx and earns just over $16,000 per year. Including overtime, Chip earned $42,000 last year working for Tyler and is on track to earn even more this year.

When Chip had entered the office earlier that evening, Tyler immediately knew that something was wrong. Chip, who is normally cheerful and energetic, looked as if he had lost his best friend. He had come to ask for the loan. He and his wife are two months behind in their lease payments on her Toyota 4Runner. She had leased the vehicle shortly after Chip began working for T&T. Chip and Mary Kay now have to come up with $480 by 2:00 p.m. the following day or her 4Runner will be repossessed.

Tyler is not completely surprised that Chip and Mary Kay are facing financial problems. The previous fall Chip had purchased a new Polaris ATV and had spent $1,500 on a new Browning shotgun. At Christmas, the couple had purchased a 50-inch Samsung flat screen television and an expensive new bedroom set. Chip had known about the unpaid lease payments for weeks. Yet he had waited until the last minute to come to Tyler with the problem.

Chip has known Tyler's family for more than 20 years. Chip seems happy in his job and is always willing to do anything Tyler asks of him at work. He never complains about the long hours that frequently are involved in the landscaping business. Tyler is certain that Chip found it difficult to come to his 24 year old boss, whom he has known since Tyler was a child, to ask for the loan.

Tyler is torn. He does not believe in loaning employees money. On two occasions since the company was founded, employees had asked for small loans: one for $100 and one for $125. Tyler did not make the loans because he did not want employees to view him as the solution to their money management problems.

Tyler had turned down several job offers when he finished college. He had always wanted to manage his own business and had risked all the money he had saved while working his way through college to start T&T.

Instead of taking money out of the company, Tyler pays himself a modest salary and plows all of the additional cash back into T&T. He is now beginning to see some of the financial rewards for his hard work and sacrifice. Earlier that week, he had completed a review of T&T's financial position and realized that he has saved enough cash to meet the working capital reserve levels needed to carry the company through the lean winter months that are coming up.

Tyler locks the doors to the office and loads Dory, his chocolate Lab, into the bed of his white 2004 Chevrolet 4x4. As he heads home, he smacks the steering wheel in frustration. Exhaustion will ensure that he falls asleep tonight as soon as his head hits the pillow. In the morning, however, after he silences the buzzing of his alarm clock at 4:30 a.m., the numbing pressure of the business will

return. On top of everything else, he will have
to deal with Chip's request for a loan. Chip
will return to work expecting an answer.

Barlow Manufacturing Company

Charles (Chuck) B. Barlow, the president of Barlow Manufacturing Company in Birmingham, Alabama, is rushing out of the company's front door, late for a business appointment. As he exits the building, he is startled to encounter a television reporter with a cameraman in tow. The reporter says, "Mr. Barlow, I am Tracy Reed with WBAL. We are interested in your views on whether Alabama should offer driver's license exams only in English."

Barlow Manufacturing Company was founded by Chuck Barlow's grandfather in the late 1930s. Chuck was the third generation of the family to head the family-owned business. His son and son-in-law, both graduates of the University of Alabama, work for the company.

The company currently has approximately 350 employees. Just over forty percent of them are immigrants, mainly from Mexico and Central America.

Since 1998, Alabama had offered the driver's license written exam in twelve languages other than English. Recently, however, five Alabama residents had sued the state to stop the practice. The five are members of ProEnglish, an organization based in Arlington, Virginia, that advocates constitutional amendments and laws that declare that English is the official language of the United States.

The question of giving written exams for drivers' licenses in languages other than English has been a political issue in Alabama and in other states since the late sixties and early seventies. The conflict pits English language advocates against civil and human rights groups and has resulted in both legislative actions and judicial suits.

In 1990, Alabama voters approved a constitutional amendment making English the state's official language. After the passage of the amendment, Alabama discontinued its practice of giving written exams for drivers' licenses in languages other than English. This resulted in legal challenges.

The American Civil Liberties Union and the Southern Poverty Law Center sued in 1996 on behalf of non-English speaking Alabama residents. This led to a series of federal court decisions that supported the plaintiffs. The U.S. Supreme Court reversed the lower courts decisions and ruled in favor of Alabama. Even so, the state decided in 1998 to offer the driver's license written exam in languages other than English.

Six states currently require that the driver's license written exams be given in English only: Alaska, Maine, New Hampshire, Oklahoma, South Dakota, and Wyoming. Maine is one of eleven states that allow undocumented immigrants to obtain driver's licenses, a practice that the U.S. Congress required states to stop by May, 2008.

K. C. McAlpin, the national executive director of ProEnglish, contends that anyone who comes to the United States should know that English is the national language and should expect to have to take the driver's license written exam in English. Furthermore, he contends that drivers who cannot read road signs in English endanger both themselves and others on the highways.

Melissa Savage, a transportation policy expert with the National Conference of State Legislatures, recognizes the argument about safety. However, she counters that there are increasing numbers of cultural groups in different communities throughout the country. "If newly arrived immigrants," she says, "don't have time to learn English, then they won't have a license.

This can lead to unlicensed drivers, which is probably a more significant safety problem than not knowing road signs."

Charles Campbell, Alabama's assistant attorney general, recently pointed out in an interview that English is Alabama's official language. However, he added, "It is not the state's only language."

Mabel Walden, a member of the Birmingham City Council, states that the basic underlying issue in the debate over giving driver's license written exams in languages other than English is not about safety. In fact, she points out that this past summer, she, her husband, and their two teenage children had traveled in a rental car through Switzerland, Germany, Austria, Italy, and France, and that none of them knew the languages of these countries. She and her husband used international driver's licenses which are easily obtained. Mrs. Walden notes that she and her husband are just two of thousands of non-native language speakers who rent cars in Europe every year and that these drivers are not menaces or special threats to highway safety while driving in Europe. The issue fueling the debate is not safety. It is opposition to immigrants coming into Alabama, especially from Latin American and Caribbean countries.

Chuck Barlow is aware that the issue of giving driver's license written exams in languages other than English is once more becoming an issue in Alabama and is receiving increasing media attention. Even so, he is surprised to find the television reporter and cameraman at the company's front entrance. He is now faced with deciding how to respond to the reporter's inquiry.

Meredith's Question about Muslim Holidays

David Stewart, a member of the Northampton County public school board, had just finished dinner when his seventh grade daughter, who had been silent throughout the meal, addressed him. Meredith asked her father, "Daddy, why don't we get out of school for Muslim kids' holy days?" Somewhat taken aback by the question, David responded, "What do you mean, honey?" Meredith replied, "Why do we have to go to school on other kids' holy days? We get off for Christmas and Easter, but we don't get off when Anyar and other Muslim students have their holy days."

David paused to consider both Meredith's question and his answer. "Well, Meredith," he said, "public schools have a set number of classroom days. If we recognize everyone's holy days, then you would have a shorter summer vacation." David hoped that his answer would satisfy his daughter's curiosity and end the conversation. He reminded her that it was time for her to get ready for bed and that if she had more questions on the subject, they could talk about it again tomorrow.

Later that evening, as David prepared for bed, he found himself pondering his daughter's question. As a member of the county's public school board, he knew that he easily could raise such a question at the next school board meeting.

David Stewart was born and raised in Northampton County, New Jersey. After high school, David attended Davidson College, a small, liberal arts school in the western piedmont of North Carolina, where he received a degree in economics. After graduating, David accepted a management position with In-Time Design (ITD), a firm in northern New Jersey.

ITD is a well-known and successful engineering consultant agency committed to a strong growth strategy. ITD has been headquartered in Northampton County since its founding in 1964.

David was very surprised when he was considered for a position with ITD, as he possessed a limited knowledge of the engineering field. ITD executives told David that the primary responsibilities associated with the position involved implementing a quality control system and recruiting top tier international talent for the company. David was offered the job.

In his first recruiting venture for ITD, David interviewed dozens of candidates. He knew that many of his peers considered candidates from the Middle East to be among the best in the engineering field.

In David's first year, ITD hired 40 Middle Eastern candidates out of a total new hire class of 64. This hiring trend continued. ITD executives believed that the highly trained Middle Eastern hires gave the company a significant competitive advantage in the engineering consulting industry.

Northampton County is located in the northeastern region of New Jersey. It is known for its rapid growth over the last few decades, the result of its proximity to New York City. Many international commercial, technology and retail industries have headquarters in Northampton County.

Northampton County has a population of 123,000 residents. Fifty-two percent of its citizens are of European descent, with English being their first language. The remaining forty-eight percent of Northampton County's population is comprised of Middle Eastern, African, and Asian ethnicities who speak, in addition to English, a wide range of native languages and dialects.

A majority of the people in Northampton County are Caucasian and have Christian or Jewish religious roots. The second most prevalent ethnic group in the county is the fast-growing Middle Eastern population, which represents twenty-two percent of the total population. Most of the members of this group claim Islamic religious affiliations.

The citizens of Northampton County are proud of their rich, diverse culture. Government officials and business leaders know that the county's demographics are directly related to its rapidly growing business sector, and they understand that the county is undergoing significant population and cultural changes.

It was Tuesday evening. A week had passed since Meredith had asked her father the question about why Muslim holy days were not recognized by her school. Her father still had the question on his mind. David approached his daughter and asked, "So, Meredith, what prompted you the other evening to ask me that question about holy days and school?" "Well, Daddy," Meredith replied, "I have Muslim friends in school, and Anyar is one of them. Last week he did not come to school for three days. When he got back, I asked if he had been sick. He told me that he had not been sick. He had been celebrating Eid ul-Fitr, which, he said, is like our Christmas holiday. He told me that Muslim families and friends get together and pray, exchange gifts and eat special foods. That made me wonder why our school does not have a break to recognize the holiday celebrations of its Muslim students."

David responded, "Meredith, you are a thoughtful girl. You must have wonderful, loving and caring parents who taught you to be aware of the feelings of others." Meredith laughed and said, "Yeah, I guess so, Daddy. But it did really make me wonder. I mean, I also have Jewish friends and our school recognizes Yom Kippur and Rosh Hashanah. So what makes Anyar and other Muslims different?"

David gave Meredith a tender look and said, "You really have been thinking about this, haven't you, darling? Well, I'll tell you what. I am going to raise the issue at the next school board meeting and let you know what everyone thinks. OK?" Pleased, Meredith responded, "That sounds great, Daddy. Thank you for listening."

The Northampton County School Board meets on the first Thursday of every month at 6:00 p.m. in the public library. School board meetings are open to the public and scheduled to last two hours, until 8:00 p.m. Board meetings follow a set agenda, with the first thirty minutes being set aside to address the past month's budget and expense report.

As the meeting was about to come to a close, David Stewart raised his hand and asked to be recognized by the chair. He addressed the other four members of the board as well as attendees. David recounted his exchange with Meredith and explained to them her concerns about the Muslim holy days. He requested that the school board members discuss the issue and asked them to weigh in with their own thoughts on recognizing the Muslim holy days as school holidays.

Martha Trent, a long-time school board member, replied, "David, I am amazed by your daughter's keen insight, and at such a young age. This is indeed an issue that requires careful consideration. Perhaps we should consider allowing our Muslim students a 'free absence' that allows them time off to celebrate the holy days with their families."

Kyle Greenberg responded, "I agree with Martha. My only question would be, where do we draw the line? If we are permitting our Muslim students time off for Islamic holy days, why not for all other religions? We must remember that as a board we are bound by state guidelines that stipulate the total number of annual classroom days required of our students. Any adjustments to the schools' schedules to recognize more religious holidays would mean that we would have to schedule makeup days to meet the required 180-day state mandated requirement."

David weighed in and made the following statement: "I have been thinking about this issue for two weeks. As you all know, I work at In-Time Design where I am responsible for, among other duties, hiring top tier professional engineers, many of whom are of Middle Eastern descent. Since Meredith approached me with her question, I have asked a number of my colleagues for their thoughts on the situation. All my Muslim colleagues agreed that such an accommodation by the public school system would be of great benefit to the Muslim community, its families, and, most of all, its children.

"One of my Muslim colleagues pointed out that several years ago Eid ul-Fitr fell on the Wednesday before the traditional American Thanksgiving holiday. He explained that this Muslim holiday includes three days of prayer and other rituals, as it marks the end of Ramadan. However, the holiday is dictated by the lunar calendar, so the actual date changes from year to year. For instance, this past year, Eid ul-Fitr fell on an in-school standard of learning test day. We all know the ramifications of missing an important test day and so do my Muslim colleagues. So what did my friend do? He sent his child to school because he did not want her to fall behind.

"Further complications include the reluctance of many of our Muslim citizens to speak out on such issues for fear of inciting a backlash from the public. As everyone here knows, since September 11, 2001, American sentiments toward Muslims have included many public declarations and manifestations of fear, anger and mistrust. Some of my Muslim colleagues simply do not want to 'stir the pot' by asking for any special privileges, even those that would seem to be guaranteed by the U.S. Constitution. As a citizen and a school board member, I do not want to play a part in depriving any of our citizens of their right to freedom of religion and speech. I simply cannot and will not allow that to happen."

"Wait a minute, David," interjected Isaiah Goldsmith, school board member and a local corporate lawyer. "I know this issue is very close to your heart, and I know that your staff of professionals at ITD is heavily populated by

Muslims. But this is not an issue of freedom of religion or freedom of speech. It is clearly an issue of the separation of church and state."

"Furthermore," added Betsy Clinghaver, "while Meredith is correct that Christmas and Easter are recognized as special holidays, they are marked as 'Winter' and 'Spring' breaks on the school system's calendar. Because of the separation of church and state, our public schools do not characterize either break as a Christian holiday."

"Your points are well taken," replied David. But what about the school system's official recognition of Yom Kippur and Rosh Hashanah? Why can't we include recognition of the holidays of the third Abrahamic faith?"

"David," said Martha Trent, "it is now 8:45 p.m. We have been talking about this for over an hour. Let us adjourn for the evening and go home and think about the issue and prepare ourselves to revisit this discussion at the next school board meeting."

They adjourn.

David knows that this is a complicated matter whose resolution, whatever it may be, will not likely sit well with everyone. Furthermore, he knows that the longer the debate drags out, the more likely more citizens will enter the fray, creating a greater likelihood for contentious exchanges to occur and feelings to be hurt. This could easily create a situation that might take on a life of its own and pollute the good will and camaraderie heretofore enjoyed by the diverse community of Northampton County.

Is it possible for the school board to structure the annual calendar to ensure that no overlaps occur between special testing days and religious holidays?

Can the school system accommodate the holidays of the major religions and still meet the 180-day classroom schedule mandated by the state?

Are the twin issues of tolerance and diversity, laudable as they are in the abstract, potential landmines that could in fact create a political climate that leads to less tolerance toward certain communities in the county's diverse population?

And what about other religions? If freedom of speech and religion are the true issues that undergird this debate, where does one, where can one draw the line? Can the public school students of Rastafarians, Wiccans,

Druids, Zoroastrians and Uyghurs press for special considerations?

And, if as Isaiah Goldsmith pointed out, the separation of church and state is the true issue here, what kind of contortions must the board go through to guarantee that holidays like Christmas and Easter are given euphemistic names like "Winter" and "Spring" break? It seems to David that even a mediocre lawyer, representing land mines of an aggrieved minority religion, could find ample cause for a lawsuit that could be very costly for the county, not only in monetary terms but in the comity between and among diverse populations that comprise the citizenry.

Four Seniors at Lafayette High

Daniel Robinson, Jesse Franklin, Corey Hernandez, and Michael Fine are rising seniors at Lafayette High School on the south side of Chicago. All four boys are close friends and rarely spend time apart. The last days of summer are coming to an end, and the four have decided to attend a career seminar hosted by their high school.

In Daniel's car on the ride to Lafayette's career seminar, the four boys talk about their plans for the future.

"So, guys," says Corey, "you think this career seminar is going to take a long time?"

"Why? What's your worry, Corey," responds Michael. "Got a date tonight?"

"Settle down, you two," interrupts Daniel. "Yes, I do think this seminar will take a long time. But look at the bright side. At least we are going to score brownie points with Principal Knox just for showing up."

"True that," adds Jesse. "Anyhow, this seminar just might help us figure out where we want to go to college. My parents have been riding my case to begin getting applications in before school starts."

"Whoa, wait a minute," protests Michael. "Who said anything about college? I have been thinking about going into the Marines like my father and uncles did."

"Well, I just want to get out of Chicago, whether it's a job, the military or college," adds Corey.

"I have no idea what I want to do after high school," says Daniel. "I just might take a year off. What do you call it? Oh yeah, a gap year. My cousin who lives in Santa Fe has a friend, and he and his buddy after graduating from high school just took off in an old car, traveling across the west and taking short-term odd jobs to support themselves. They worked in Durango, Jackson Hole, Sun Valley, and at a saw mill in some small town in Oregon. Then they went north, took the Alaskan Highway, and worked on a fishing boat up there. I don't know what they learned, but they sure had fun."

"I guess that is a possibility, just take off for a year," Jessie says. "I certainly have no idea what I want to do next year. But it's time we seriously think about where we are headed after high school. This career seminar might be a complete waste of time, but then again it might be a good thing. It can't hurt."

It is the first year that Lafayette High School is hosting a summer career seminar, and administrators and faculty members are hoping that the event will be a success. The purpose of the seminar is to help current students "find and pursue their passions in life at an early age." College and military representatives, local business recruiters, and others had been invited to speak at the seminar. Administrators at Lafayette High want their students, especially their seniors, to be challenged to think about their futures and the many options open to them.

During the seminar, the word "success" turns out to be a focal point for many of the speakers. As the moderator notes, "Success is a relative term. What is considered success for one person may be considered a failure for another."

To illustrate the point further, the moderator hands out three by five inch index cards to audience members and asks each attendee to write on the card his or her definitions of "a successful life." As anticipated by the career seminar speakers, the definitions vary widely and focus on different goals: money, power, happiness, adventure, prestige, good health, a strong family life, and serving others.

The moderator asks for volunteers from among the rising seniors in attendance to read their definitions of "a successful life" to the entire audience. Daniel, Jesse, Corey, and Michael raise their hands and are among the ten who are chosen.

Daniel: "My definition of a successful life is one where I am outside every day, and I make a good enough living to have a happy family."

Jesse: "A successful life for me includes going to college and making a lot of money."

Corey: "A successful life for me would be filled with travel, adventure, and helping people."

Michael: "Success for me involves entering the military, specifically the Marine Corps, where I would be in charge of a lot of other Marines, and marrying a Victoria's Secret model." The audience laughs.

The other rising seniors chosen to read their statements offer their thoughts on a successful life, most of which are similar to those given by Daniel, Jesse, Corey, and Michael.

After hearing from the other students, the moderator thanks all the seniors for volunteering. One of the speakers then says,

"Let us analyze some of these definitions in a little detail. In fact, let us play a game and try and match a career to each of the seniors' definitions of a successful life." The speaker, with help from the audience, suggests the following career possibilities for Daniel, Jesse, Corey, and Michael.

For Daniel: Suggestions include entering a park ranger program or becoming a crane operator. Both of these jobs require the successful completion of training programs and are open to anyone 18 years or older.

For Jesse: Suggestions focus on looking into four-year colleges and choosing careers in industrial sales, business management and/or law. The discussion also emphasizes that making a lot of money and going to college do not always coincide.

For Corey: Suggestions heavily favor joining the Peace Corps or Teach for America. Other options include becoming a physician's assistant or entering the hospitality management field.

For Michael: Suggestions favor a military career, possibly coupled with a four-year degree with a major in leadership or management. Audience members add that Michael could possibly get the Marines to pay for a college education.

The final speaker rises to conclude the career seminar with a quote stressing the meaning of "a successful life." She says, "The keys to a successful life are identifying your passions, what makes you happy, and taking the necessary steps to integrate these passions into your daily lives."

She continued: "I have not come here today to tell you what to do. Rather, I have come here today to challenge you to think about your futures and what you want to do with your lives. Some of you will go directly into the workforce; others will go to a technical school, a community college, or a four-year bachelor's program; some will enter the military; and one of you might even marry a Victoria's Secret model upon graduation from high school. I wish you the best, but I also challenge you to find your passion and experience 'a successful life.'"

As the four boys climb back into Daniel's car to go to McDonald's for hamburgers, they are kidding Michael about his Victoria's Secret model comment. Looking at Michael, Daniel says, "Well, you surely got a laugh about what you wrote on your card. I guess it is okay to dream, but there should be some reality to the dream."

Jesse interrupts the playful banter: "Did you guys look at the sheets they had for us to pick up?"

"What sheets?" asked Corey.

"The ones that were on the table outside the auditorium door," responds Jesse. "Look at this. Here is a guy who is making over $1,000,000 a year" (see Exhibit 1). "That appeals to me. That's a lot more than a Marine private makes, and I bet this guy doesn't eat at McDonald's or drive a beat-up old Ford. And look at this second sheet about the benefits of college." Jesse begins to read aloud the differences in salaries and unemployment rates between college graduates versus high school graduates (see Exhibit 2).

"That all sounds good on paper," says Corey. "But I wonder how happy those guys with big salaries are. They might make lots of money, but I bet they don't have time for hunting, fishing, and just hanging out."

Exhibit 1

What People Earn
A Look at Selected Jobs from around the U.S.

Job	City	State	Age	Income
Elementary Teacher	Maytown	PA	29	$34,000
Construction Worker	Aberdeen	SD	25	$21,500
Army Private	Fairbanks	AK	19	$19,464
Fishing Boat Crewperson	Nags Head	NC	23	$16,800
Shepherd	Caldwell	ID	39	$13,900
Sporting Goods Clerk	Freeport	ME	28	$17,700
Cement Truck Driver	Beckley	WV	36	$32,000
Architect	Meza	AZ	52	$130,000
Boat Mechanic	Key West	FL	64	$38,000
Instructional Designer	Chapel Hill	NC	34	$42,700
Residential Electrician	Hope	AR	44	$30,500
Minister	Greenville	SC	53	$61,000
UPS Pilot	Cincinnati	OH	48	$144,000
Bulldozer Operator	Ulysses	KS	46	$30,000
Registered Nurse	St. Cloud	MN	58	$65,000
Bicycle Mechanic	Cincinnati	OH	31	$28,700
Pizza Delivery Person	Frederick	MD	21	$23,900
Investment Banker	New York	NY	28	$1,350,000
Locksmith	Taos	NM	48	$38,000

Tobacconist	Oxford	MS	53	$46,200
Astrologer	Las Vegas	NV	52	$163,000
College Football Coach	Austin	TX	36	$1,100,000
Firefighter	Bloomington	IN	27	$55,000
Management Consultant	Taunton	MA	48	$158,000
Speech Pathologist	Glen Ridge	NJ	37	$87,000
Lawyer	Columbia	SC	51	$152,000
Business Development Manager	Stamford	CT	34	$105,000
Appliance Delivery Person	Rochester	NY	40	$38,500
High School Teacher	Bellingham	WA	27	$39,200
Carpenter	Georgetown	DE	31	$37,800
Singer	Nashville	TN	33	$8,400,000
Farm Equipment Mechanic	Tupelo	MS	45	$27,000
Pediatric Nurse	Memphis	TN	39	$69,000
Long-Distance Truck Driver	Seymour	IN	23	$38,000
Ski Patroller/Carpenter	Crested Butte	CO	35	$39,000
Paramedic	Elizabeth	NJ	45	$50,000
Air Traffic Controller	Atlanta	GA	43	$109,200
Peace Corp Volunteer	Carson	NV	22	$2,900
IT Project Manager	Wellesley	MA	54	$135,000
Deputy Sheriff	Jamestown	MO	41	$34,500
Farm Worker	Seaboard	NC	37	$22,500
Certified Public Accountant	Hilo	HI	47	$79,000

Rodeo Steer Wrestler	Dalhart	TX	26	$138,000
College Professor	Granville	OH	53	$74,000
Surgeon	Naperville	IL	37	$765,000
United States Senator	Washington	DC	58	$174,000
Software Engineer	Dover	NH	54	$87,000
Obituary Writer	Arcadia	CA	57	$65,300
Tow Truck Driver	Bismarck	ND	25	$39,000
Musician	Portland	OR	22	$13,500
Meat Packer Worker	Storm Lake	IA	28	$17,800
Supreme Court Justice	Washington	DC	77	$213,900
Artist	Janesville	WI	50	$38,400
Rancher	Lamar	CO	64	$41,000
Chief Executive Officer	Houston	TX	63	$31,400,000
Sawmill Worker	Carrsville	VA	19	$15,600
Oil Well Driller	Beaumont	TX	25	$66,300
City Sustainability Manager	Oak Park	IL	43	$72,000
Excavator	Tulsa	OK	29	$37,000
College Football Line Coach	Athens	GA	47	$750,000
Medical Grant Administrator	Bend	OR	55	$57,000
Equity Manager	San Francisco	CA	43	$5,600,000
Physical Trainer	Cranston	RI	40	$39,000
Professional Football Player	Minneapolis	MN	32	$16,000,000
Motorcycle Mechanic	Richfield	UT	29	$16,000

City Bus Driver	Washington	DC	40	$56,000
Plastic Surgeon	Houston	TX	42	$1,300,000
Motel Manager	Bennington	VT	32	$39,000
Park Ranger	Columbia Falls	MT	33	$32,000
Mortgage Officer	Cary	NC	41	$77,000
Physical Therapist	Birmingham	AL	39	$71,100
Veterinarian	Oklahoma City	OK	44	$141,000
Industrial Electrician	Newport News	VA	47	$79,000
Miner	Somerset	CO	30	$60,000
Fork Lift Operator	St. Louis	MO	20	$40,000
News Reporter	Madison	WI	33	$29,400
Lifeguard	Nags Head	NC	24	$9,000
Machine Operator	Huntington	WV	39	$52,500
Graphic Illustrator	Bennington	VT	36	$36,400
Tattooist	Grand Rapids	MI	28	$49,700
Construction Foreman	Lewiston	ID	41	$48,000
President of the United States	Washington	DC	49	$400,000
Postal Clerk	Dalhart	TX	52	$54,500
Medical Record Transcriber	Yankton	SD	64	$26,000
Administrative Assistant	San Jose	CA	30	$25,500
Home Builder Contractor	Naples	FL	58	$118,000
Assembly Line Worker	Lansing	MI	59	$41,000
Waitress	St. Joseph	MO	18	$15,300

Aircraft Mechanic	Portland	ME	44	$54,900
Auctioneer	Denver	CO	47	$184,000
Logistics Manager	Kansas City	MO	38	$155,000
Supermarket Clerk	New Orleans	LA	38	$20,100
Paralegal	Louisville	KY	34	$55,000
Bricklayer	Manchester	NH	33	$33,300
Navy Captain	Norfolk	VA	35	$105,000
Car Sales Manager	Cincinnati	OH	34	$178,000
Radio Producer	Providence	RI	38	$85,000
Anesthesiologist	Rochester	MN	45	$368,000
Lawn Care Worker	Miami	FL	19	$14,720
Loan Officer	Gadsden	AL	27	$71,000
Pediatrician	Dallas	TX	38	$205,000
Locomotive Engineer	Birmingham	AL	35	$84,000
Roofer	Fargo	NC	49	$35,900
Hedge Fund Manager	New York	NY	43	$89,000,000
Pipe Fitter	Seattle	WA	37	$48,800
Ranch Manager	Guyman	OK	52	$51,300
Bakery Clerk	Westport	CT	26	$18,900
Industrial Salesperson	Arrow	OH	58	$210,000
Police Officer	Greenwich	CT	32	$62,000
Paralegal	Sioux Falls	SD	28	$31,000

Exhibit 2
Things to Think About

Annual Median Income by Level of Education

- Less than a High School Diploma: $23,600
- High School Diploma: $32,600
- Some College: $37,800
- Bachelor's Degree: $53,300
- Advanced Degree: $69,100

Annual Unemployment Rates by Level of Education

- Less than a High School Diploma: 15.6%
- High School Diploma: 10.5%
- Some College: 8.0%
- Bachelor's or Advanced Degree: 5.0%

Over the past ten years, the cost of college tuition and fees have increased by 92%. During this same period, the cost of medical care has increased by 49%; the cost of food, by 32%; and the cost of automobiles, by less than 1%.

By the age of 33, the typical four-year college graduate who enrolled in a public university at age 18 will have earned enough to compensate for being out of the work force for four years and to pay tuition and fees without grant aid.

What's the Point?

William Hargrave had gone through all of the motions and had ended up exactly where he had intended. Nonetheless, he feels a vast void in his life. He finds himself torn and in emotional upheaval at the realization that he no longer knows what it was exactly that he wants or needs.

At the age of 12, William was already planning his life. His father instilled in him the drive and determination to achieve goals that closely matched the path the father himself had followed.

After graduating *summa cum laude* from Georgetown University, his father's alma mater, William followed in his father's footsteps and joined the U.S. Army, ultimately serving five years and rising to the rank of Captain.

Upon the completion of his military service, William entered the M.B.A. Program of the Harvard Business School. Although confident in his intellectual capabilities and leadership, he experienced, during his first days at Harvard, a nagging sense of hesitancy. His unease was soon put to rest, however, as he found his niche in graduate school and reclaimed his confidence.

William worked on Wall Street during the summer between his first and second years at Harvard. By November of his second year in graduate school, he had received five competitive offers from financial institutions. After carefully evaluating his options, William accepted the job offer from The International Bank of the Americas.

William finished at the top of the training class at The International Bank of the Americas, a significant achievement given that he was competing against peers from other prestigious business schools, such as Harvard, Pennsylvania, Michigan, Northwestern, Chicago, and Stanford. William's skills in finance earned him the respect and admiration of his peers and senior management. William loved his work, performed exceptionally, and was the first to be awarded a multi-million dollar portfolio of commercial customers in the heart of the most competitive banking market in the country, New York City.

During his first year, the able but unseasoned young banker scrambled for new business. He consistently logged 90 to 100 hour weeks that were only intermittently broken up by the occasional Sunday off, most of which he spent in front of the television, sleeping out of utter exhaustion.

William employed every resource at his disposal and remained steadfast in his efforts to grow his book of business. His relentless pursuits began to pay off. At the close of the first year, William was rewarded for his labors with a whopping six-figure bonus, along with a promotion to Vice President, making him one of the youngest VPs in the history of the bank.

After a hefty chunk of his bonus went to Uncle Sam, William put a large down payment on his first home. He used the remainder to purchase the engagement ring he had chosen for his supportive and extremely patient girlfriend, Heather.

William's second year at the bank was made memorable by his and Heather's wedding, which was followed by their honeymoon that was cut from ten days to five in order for William to complete a pending deal. At the end of his second year at the bank, William received an unexpectedly large bonus for the outstanding growth of his portfolio. Of course, this last bit of success came with a cost: even more hours spent at the office, hours not spent with his wife or on his own health and well-being. While on the surface William was living the great American dream of professional and financial success, he could not help but feel that he was a failure in his personal life. Even in the limited time he had to share with Heather, William could see clearly that his wife was becoming unhappy.

William suddenly found himself at an impasse. His success at the bank had only raised expectations and put more pressure on him for future performance. And he knew that his assigned performance goals would surely increase for the upcoming year. Although the bank promotes a work/life balance in its recruiting materials, William knows that his job is driven solely by "the bottom line." He knows too that he can expect little sympathy from management and peers if he asks for time off for personal reasons. He fears that he is too young and too new to the game to be in crisis. This is simply not how disciplined over-achievers behave.

William mulls over a variety of scenarios involving how he might best meet the demands of his job, while continuing to earn his father's respect and somehow address the conflicts he has with the needs of his personal life.

William often seeks momentary escape at times of great pressure by letting his mind drift to his happiest days, training SCUBA divers for the Army. He recalls the euphoria of those long-ago afternoons: being bathed by the sun, with the refreshing tropical breezes delivering a delicate bouquet from local flora and the enchanting melodies of the long-legged warblers native to the region. In these reveries, William allows himself to be transported to the crystal blue waters of the tropics. He attains a Zen-like state as he imagines the fluid movements of the underwater acrobatics he and his trainees performed, such beauty, such effortless grace, all choreographed by the gods, it seemed.

Unfortunately, these calming memories will not lead him to a solution to his anxieties and looming depression. Reality always looms.

As William gazes out his office window, he thinks, "What's the point?"

The cases you have just explored
are about people, much like you,
who are on journeys yet to be completed.
May you continue to travel with the thoughtful insight, strong
integrity, enriching curiosity,
and invigorating passion required to create the values and
informed actions that define
lives of influence and impact.

About the Author

Edward L. Felton, Jr. has had a thirty-five year career in management teaching, research, and consulting in the areas of ethics, strategy, and economic development. He has authored or co-authored eight books and more than two hundred and fifty management case studies and articles.

Dr. Felton currently is Professor of Business Administration at the Mason School of Business at the College of William and Mary and heads the School's Walsh Ethics Initiative. Prior to his current positions, he was the Margaret Gage Bush University Professor at Samford University, dean and professor of management at the Babcock School of Management at Wake Forest University, and a member of the faculties of The Darden School of Business at the University of Virginia and the Harvard Business School. Dr. Felton also was a member of teams that established five graduate schools of management overseas. His professional activities have taken him to more than seventy-five countries, and he has conducted management seminars in over thirty-five countries.

Dr. Felton has worked with a variety of domestic and international private and public sector organizations. These include Citicorp, Champion International, Eskom, Continental Grain, Cooper & Lybrands, The Southern Company, The Aspen Institute, the United States Department of State, The Ford Foundation, The Rockefeller Foundation, and The World Bank.

Dr. Felton earned his doctoral and master degrees in business administration at Harvard University. He received a

Bachelor of Divinity degree from Southeastern Seminar and a Bachelor of Arts degree from the University of Richmond where he was elected to Phi Beta Kappa, Omicron Delta Kappa and Tau Kappa Alpha.

To contact the author: edward.felton@mason.wm.edu.

Previous Works by Edward L. Felton, Jr.

Leadership for Business Results

Managerial Decision-Making: A Ten-Step Process

Agroindustria en Centroamerica: Respuesta al Cambio
(with Roberto Artavia)

Managerial Perspectives on Agricultural Research
(with S. Huntington Hobbs IV)

Private Sector Participation in Agricultural Development:
Perspectives and Opportunities
(with John C. Edmunds)

Agribusiness in Iran: Opportunities for Investment

Managerial Decision-Making
(with John B. Bennett)

Agribusiness Management for Developing
Countries—Latin America
(with Ray A. Goldberg)

www.ingramcontent.com/pod-product-compliance
Lightning Source LLC
Chambersburg PA
CBHW021340090426
42742CB00008B/675